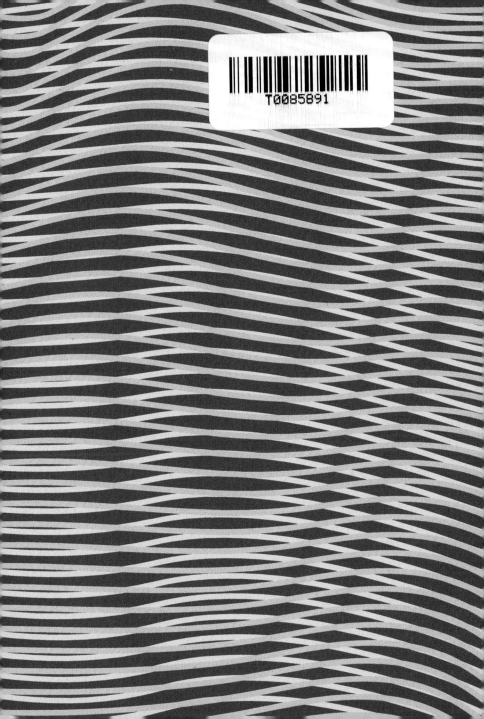

ECHO'S ERRAND

Keith Jones

Black Ocean
Boston · Chicago

ISBN: 978-1-939568-51-9

Library of Congress Control Number: 2022933041

FIRST EDITION

Printed in Canada

para mi madre

and

in memory of

my father
Robert William Jones
1934–2008

and

mi abuela
Felicia Fernandez
1914–2005

and

my sister
Carleene Jones
1962–2013

and

William Corbett
1942–2018

and

Laura Townsend
1934–2009

and

my nephew and godson
Ryan Daniel Nessi
1990–2022

Echo thus lets be heard by whoever wants to hear it, by whoever might love hearing it, something other than what [he or she, they or it] seems to be saying

— Jacques Derrida

to be blown into fragments. your death
like the islands that you loved
like the seawall that you wished to heal

— Kamau Brathwaite

if rigor is our dream

— Hortense Spillers

CONTENTS

1

1

WEIGHTLESS CLUTCH OF SEA

I see woven
things celestial, you say, prodigious
ridden out to task, pro-
fuse, line by line
gnawing at the wind's keep
taut plane of arrival, sewn
fangs kept for feasting
broadcloth   caught,
loose mesh, weave
we call season
weightless clutch of sea,
calabash thick as alabaster
as fountain pen, as seeds
devouring time, forms slip past
prior to, pieces of,
drying   in the co-matter
of light

LUCIDITIES SUBTLY NOTCHED

waves   a fundament emphatic, undergird
　　　the airily whole, scarlet dance
at noontime   *arithmetic*
　　　if straight lines tidy
the time of death here, she says,
　　　　we glimpse eternity's jagged edge, here
we feel crab ward   the steady-unsteady
　　　way of animations,
lucidities subtly notched.
　　　warm care felt at, felt towards,
all unities in transit,
　　　under, unto, a finite will un-
done   return'd to, flush'd out, washed ashore
　　　again, calm'd —
you, aggrieved not
　　　by lost references

CLOTHED IN CROSSROADS

      a simple touch, or stitch, temper's ricochet
in close-up   fixed grip
      of clot, of being's debt
which cools the fevers of night.
      there, where the middle sea
began,   battered relics appear
      geographic, clothed in crossroads, the buoyant,
heard, adrift   wound
      upon the water, the long hold of blues
in shadow, the we

IS SINKING, LEAKING LIFE

       a quiet shade: paint

me wide, oceanic

      you say, tear

& tear,

       surface effects —

milk-blood beauty,

      dawn's

fright-full

     keep

ECHO OF OUR INMOST EDGES

err is not a word, what rises,
an invisible estate
aslant in long missives.
you say, clouds, time's hand-
cuff, referents without
a point of view.
you stitch dark planks
of white night together,
hum the great sphere,
the faint summons
of delicate surmise
the All told in peer
& limb, echo
of our inmost edges
variations we see,
ear to window, of lilting
diaphanous light.
I see the sea thru you, you say,
fleets of open
broken vessel

LANGUAGE SIGHING TO ITSELF

say, it is language

sighing to itself

a sentence, in longhand, long prior to letters,

chalk tied to beauty's tail.

reluctance spun, daylight's

pointed beak, pointing

where? eager

the arrow is eager, the emperor

is eager to sketch

his shadow

WILD LIPS A WOUND

     arisen echo of furthest edge
argent, yr wild lips a wound, a swollen incision
     surface effects shredded to mute, frantically thinned
like a dead man forever talking,
     never saying a word he meant, chatter-worn,
as the wound over the actual
grows fonder more profuse, bridles a bit
     a torrent now, this prized cut,
this creased propellant, where need's tremor
     spills out, drips, seeps presses up some rusty ledge
in you, you crawl, you slip, you over-
     state the sparse
till'd passage, the graven burrow
     you still flounder in

voyages forgetting asymmetric

aerialist stove, warmth in deeper recesses,

you say, abandoned, sink, rise,

surface again, list the haggard craft mono-chromatic, no
longer in luck —

of his ilk antiphony, a new renewal delayed

long kept in pretty snares, bursts which loosen,

which recall the pretty waves, she says

of beauty's wake, airily made

barks cutting   arcs

in water

LIFTS AN ARCHAIC CURSE

no palm'd tree, no laurel, no swan,
you are sharp feeling   rushed exit-
less fall   ark life to infidel, like speech to stutter,
lifts an archaic curse   note how day's
encumbrance took eons, she sd.
hammer'd thin, fine crater lake
light, oblique   hoofbeat's mad rush
fumes of final days, turning
you, yes, contemporary,
most alive, drifting up, from long
ago, on bone-white night   you,
like radio, you, like song

you soften me,
strip me bare, which is why I like
yr white cliffs best,
balled into paper-whites
a plinth   beginnings
echo revenant echo
forms echo prow stern keel
blue streak of oar
bled thru   all aspects of

enter walls, discrepant waves, back-
bone of seeing's boat   hoofbeat,
        beat slap of skin
lost at sea   sea is West
        where sunset is,   sea is
the weary need
        of feather, of wood where I, too,
look entire

                to float

IN A FIELD OF FALSE TIME

no cure, ornery,
first language,
then not   then nothing
wrists elaborately bound,
dissolves, little
by little, she says
a field of false time
it's not worth explaining
what ritual does not preserve
my voice
scribbles it

DAZED WITH WHAT
WE THINK WE KNOW

dazed with what we think we know
Adonis recedes,
repeats a world-style   no more
"Petals of Fire" endlessly
muttering ... to re-invent
is elliptical, fleshy republic
of feeling   grey crossings,
Marrakech

THE IMPERIAL CITY SURROUNDS,
ITS HISTORY SO BLUE

the imperial city surrounds,
its history so blue, slurs
my lust for you, Naumachia
middle sea, middle passage,
mechanical, blind oceanic way
man overboard, woman over-
board, thrown, still thrown
leaping

UPBRAIDED, BURNT BY FIRE

medusa & ovum, she says
blood bloom
the drowning siege
of various waters
an eyelid,
an eagle's crest,
floating shades
& bounded nests,
worsted aftermath
of Iliam
on & on,
wings thinned,
upbraided, burnt
by fire

OF SHORE & GRIEF

for William Corbett

        wheels crayons house-
paint suddenly
        panoramic,   chalk on walls,
ol' equestrian battles
        the wine-chosen edge, you say
is.social light, is fine snow
        to fountain, is
molecular
        to these dark waters
audible the trap
        the solitude, leagues
beneath you, un-
        mourned

"A" is for Achilles,　　his circumferences,
flight in pure space.
　　imagine you are all interval,
pursued, pierced, halo'd in veils of sea
　　in veils of sand　in veils

of shore & grief

& speed   "the islands that you loved"

combed out, internal

in these strains

of beauty's summons, slow

wheel to steady, creaks

eternal having been given to peaks,

the fortress

is hard to find, craft's

taut curve

stretched thin

the thing you pluck,

        lattices like rigging

spines of leaves stones thrown,

        mystic sigh skip,   you say

old man is I,   little cloud is I, youth's

        craned waves

incandescent

        sweet tensile strength,

my love for you, sweet grass, cliff's

        kiss,

the jagged limb'd

        coronations of

color

CLUTCH OF EMBLEMATIC SHORE

yr work had been to white-out yr capital,
center of yr city

cut its rigging, let it
float out & up & away.

vanish in-
to a butterfly's kiss. orange wings, clutch

of emblematic shore. clap yr hands
& it flies away

its fine art an envelope
you say it was

the disappearance of
a strong kind

of runaway feeling, diamond hard,
its wattage flickering

wild workhorse of night
fencepost, doorknob,

window ledge
& frame, you tease this thicket

depth mad as autumn,
where letters lie

interrupted,
wander off   full-stop & period

half-moon boats,
erudite   lunar flesh

descending, crane'd
against the waves

a relics crate,
of sea reach

afloat,
a pool
of light

LETTERS SETTLING LIKE BLACK BIRDS, THEN SCATTER

wields the line
so wearily,
mired in the never
you are, begun again
long weary lines, you say,
I unrest you
black bird,
where the white
tread is,
skimming
the shores
of the nu-
minous

BLOWN RAKE OF TEARS

or do they, or are they, she says,
confessions
    from above?
loss you can do
    little with,
bent long-
    ways in-
to silence,   silence
    worsens the roar,
wake of wave,
    blown rake
of tears
    Xenophon's
swirling loss

            ten thousand
men, attuned
            to the void. a tired
            cry   thick
the cause,
            war's inexhaustible
echo.
            "four Black girls,"
Kitty Genovese,
            napalm. cruel mounds
where the heart-wrench
            is, where wrong
is, where wrong
            lies in fields
& seas, un-
            buried

IN THE DARK WATERS BELOW

how language
& line repeat
in dark waters below
Ottoman & Christian,
oarsmen soldiers slaves,
loosened like,
leaking life,
Lepanto, 1571

OF SEA & TWISTED KELP

"The singer and the sea, all things are moved by love."
— Osip Mandelstam

1

graced by some secret border,
time's pretty cuff

feeling travel
loosen

bones give way,
lost verse horses

2

crumples yr paper cup
tiny hinge

the hollow
in the blur of you —

the sums you give
I screw to you,

feel yr breasts,
steal yr radius & heat

3

I herd yr flowers
into hills

my voice
yr glittering

address. skin
to skin,

I sense grace
in you, my perfect

kin. wolf
heart in you,

eat
my harness,

the hold I'm
in

4

traces that remain,
dark sky in its royal

slumber loop
you will never

reach
I atmosphere you

brush & bristle
loss you seep

an intimation
of, depth of one

falling into
the other

5

you take me,
nymph of time's dis-

temper, *prima facie*
shore & tide

bank of sums
you give

in this blur,
yr incumbent mask

in this echo, you give,
& give again —

me, she says,
my voice

SHADE OF, BOUND TO YOU

    bound to you   too elliptical
what the sun will efface   in a different motif
plainest of threads   speak of yr renewal   the sky is a which seed
that blooms   washes away   cleans
    is silence   a crisp bed sheet   canvas   page
overboard & overbearing   the leaping is inside
    you   yr hurt   faraway   the eyes'll face   entangled fields
the sea   the first
    experiment   no fences if desire is   no fences make do

you let gold return
to   un quicksilvered parts   to feldspar   to blind river way
    let it sink   back in   to earth   to burn bright
alone   among roots   quiet grubs & clusters

you who miss nocturnal light   passional underground stars
warmth in what it is   descending
   a shiver   frail   it keeps in voyage   salt-flake'd shimmering
   skin
don't you remember   *is sinking*   man overboard   yr swollen
lamb
   open most
bursting within   sunk under the weight of testimony   lavish
foam,
   "X"   where middle sea began   swimmer not yet free
a wind forever panting   perishing   final facts   there
   where myth went
massive   what the page won't take   weary of its own echo
   wake in fur
wake again   here,   you clutch at Euripides
   moon at quarter-mast

ravish this   indigo island air   summer's wheeling
    advance
crinkling stubbled earth   to lean on
    a vanishing line
heteroclite   reeds
    in the dying light
of holy water   the old problem of the present is new

straying   cloud men

seized by the happy short life of labor

    of sense   blind to you

"woman" you say   old   sail   cloth   her pronoun

    yellowing   watch   how the moon slicks

the river way   mirrors   what will is   will creeps through

    topples its virgin self   as old ways

of earth   cluster round

    as present crafts conceal you   as tidal winds reach

further in & out   woven child

rags make you coast

    thru salt & twisted kelp   wishing too much

    voyage proof   this century

    terror white

SHORN ELLIPSES

while I fall away the grandeur alas
shrinks yr stare's
visage, a fountain-
full of thoughts. it's having been
there, by yr side
forgotten, arches through which
where weeds once were
were now but love's
bouquet. the now of whimsy's
bequest.
after all, of much
decision, a promise,
the paradigm's
lovely hoax. so you say again,
& do again,
& go hard after

the bristling hope. polish the sky,
pristine little shoes you walk the heavens with.
of course, you cannot bear what you
cannot hold, apostrophes
& their matters
of possession
which ask of you,
of all those things
you cannot bear — love
love love — I dare
you

2

THROWN BEYOND MEASURE

how long here, dwelling
    in yr striations,
some far here I see
    in you
intervals.

    the motion is upwards,
thrown beyond
    measure.
a land leashing you
    to its seasons,

to its Orrery,
to its settled dis-
        enchantment,
beyond what the aerialist does, shakes
        out uncertain
forms, cracks the rift
        dire   to escape

over head
out side
the spangled net
of now
some daze
& blur, she says
some through whom ablaze
in its scattering
some scattering
half gone this way goes
to what is not
bound by breath,
some horizon —
in her hair

of course, these forces
forge, teach
the tips
to touch
not by Balkan light,
more Adriatic.
a light that blurs
in supposed loss

              its proof
brings fire,
              heat of many barrels
clouds in the other
              river   where rouge
hinges
              last acts
of day

PERCEPTION'S FARAWAY DOOR

shells preceding
the starship,
pricked by perception's
faraway   door
outer banks   of Cassiopeia.
we who sing   to shatter,   our shelter,
off-key

sprawl, wave
threshold wench   diving to salvage
the sturdy bell
that swells
its torn gown
shimmering with broken bits,
spindly smashed aeons,   here
atthefoot
oftheladder

IN THE LURE OF SORROW

        we assemble, you say
these bearings
        while axe blades wish
to quiver,
        angles roost
not needing so much,
        slow to lift.
if fire does not forge
        where occasionally it darkens
to light,
        there,
in the lure
        of sorrow,
leave
        yr relics
unnamed

SINGED WING

silver'd oval, island of glass
measure, or share,
not of consequence.
white winds of winter,
I believe in the possibility
of sun, she says
I've no belief

SHEET MUSIC

1

you listen long enough
& wander long enough
 & wait.
as godsends accumulate
 or don't. did
as aerialists will
 will the air to give way —
one thinks of siblings,
 speedboats, long waves redundant
blue barrier,
 blue
beneath

2

 & then there was water
a barrage of grief
 glyph in the middle, multiple,
& staggering.

I give this machine

to you, she says. stolen bright god

skin's raiment of wonder

not so, wherever,

where the ladder leads.

because fires rage,

pleats upon the water.

washed up on shore

of day,

a minor

new world

among us

3

let accident

be everything

all at once,

rough Paradiso of day.

some force

shoreward in-
    side, coeval,
lantern you drew
    in the chiaroscuro
of intimate

4

    you say applaud
I say rebuttal,
    folded animal
circumference
    near gravel, near grain.
a songbird's plume
    you cannot command

5

you went
where the young ore was
adrift
upon a mercy, a phenom-
enon distinctly plaited,
like solar light
hammered thin
there is nothing here gigantic
eliminata, mob-
rule, you,
of grass blade & sun bridge,
of midge & mote,
one long
molecular beam, on
this island
of print

BLUEST DOME

> "The world is gone, I have to carry you."
> — Paul Celan

      angles   island   inlaid   lay in glass
but of night,   you were
     the sparest root, un-
accountably in
     solitude,
acutest   seeker a god-
     send of flock, she says
of copper stalks, of embers atop
     yr castle's keep, phan-
tasmatic, you say
     an empire's
wall
     of grief

I CRY IN CIRCUITS, SHE SAYS

body is first breath,
an envoy where a sheltering un-
encumbers itself

when the pyre dies,
laden the Urn.
the rim of it,

over the lip, you say
a spinning breech.
I've learned

of yr betrayals
of yr arrivals in abbreviation,
yr phantasms effaced

clutch of indigo,
reeds in the dying light
of holy water

ROOT WORD, LITURGICAL TETHER

the likened part of exile,
the pricked edge,
the old wharf's
endangerments —
ferrying you inward, you say
outside yr window

root word, liturgical tether
as if yr mirrors float
irresistibly beneath
faint petals night ochre
borealis,

   lunar-tinged

peak.

   come to me,

sweet peonies

   in this second life

I leave letters

   for you

primal, you say,

   as pretty

cleave

   as stone

YR WOUNDED GODS

        wondrous   still weather
home wings singed
      by any means
some portrait of
      yr wounded gods,
an echo
      you see things, too
you say,

        in back of that
our world
        feathers you pluck
from parting clouds
        diagonal clusters,
evangelical light
        a kettle pond
entitled to un-
        knowing, harbors
a marbled
        stake

BLUE DEPOSITS

       creak spine of surface
I, with gusts,
       concerning sensations
double breath, hidden
       animals,   I was reference,
you murmured,
       blue fluidity
of voice, you

       she sd., could prosper, too

. in contemplation

       leaving yr distances

whole,

       way of, lucid well,

lapidary

       useless truth,

cave,   length

       of vessel

DUSK WATER LIGHT

I have poured over that
& you — hated
how honest the torrent is
& let it be mine
not sheltered   neither poplar
nor linden
the shade shattering
just where you left
& I wonder
in advance
& cannot wait —
painting the phosphorescent side
of leaves   where mind
& cloud
make page

       & I sail my own

trans-

       figurations, you say — these

long time ago,

       a pyre, as crisp

curtailment ful-

       fills   belief

EMBED UNSPOOL BAROQUE

like tiered under edges
I asked you
not to be my god,
to huddle with me.
where the echo
of all that's ever been said,
our most recent
extinction

you asked,
how does one arrive there
improper?
edges to which

I no doubt touch
as sound cuts out —
    how wondrous yr city of meaning
& trace
    a watermark
as petals,
        & so I say, "permit,"
Cathar, winnowing's
    seat,
wait for no occasions
    of mourning

REFT GROUND

a star in her ignited a little rose
more than what theology names
bound to no epistle
a covenant that broods,
declares itself a nursery.
nebulous what one finds
said difficulties in — that things
do occur & do so birth
& will

A PICTURE BOOK

for Fanny Howe

1.1

apricot & orange, dying willow,
it is just the sky, you say
shy blue surrounding clouds

1.2

they are vermillion, twilight's shift
daystar's final tear,
scar unfolding a crippled gaze

1.3

an oracle's bleeding penance, such is
the primrose fading
child-like wish on the altar of West

PERMISSION IS NOT WHAT I ASK OF YOU

permission is not what I ask of you
the great wandering is into the interior
I try to think in singulars, she says
in numbers long
since expired,
& you are one of those impossibilities,
a lucid upward ladder

it is all proximity, listless, misspent.
as circles tide into theorems,
why thief
my miracles from me?
in the realm of my own uncertainty,
in my own
upward draft

where wind was first
to walk on water
I remain with you /
a misadventure.
I sleep, I avail
all further witnessing
these animal cone dwellings that depart,
upturn feet to flames
it is a corona
of deep breathing, you say, in these matters of devotion.
if only our exhalations could cut
a hole   through the Wishes
we expose
as gulls unspool / cross in *kenebowe*
haul the sea air in
quiet engine,
the crag trim
ocean

shot through
　　　barnacled, brown
-flecked
　　　in-
land we lay

DAYLIGHT, QUOTIDIAN

were this not to intrude
upon yr valences, she says,
some warrant caressed,
held like an idol
echoes enframed,
a double,
dire wistful
bunch
bluest cloud
covering us, you say
bluest spruce of us
we keep

if you were not here
in my ambivalence
            I'd walk through
this halo
            to the anchor below,
orange in Valencia's
            Coptic light,
saturated
            as you descend
in god's giving jewel,
            in gardens that lead
to the sea

WEAVE WOVEN GOD SO EAST

they are already there –
hidden away   gravestone,
flagstone, silhouette
a pebble falls is recurrent

fragments of increments
of memories
Elysium is in the strange respects
you pay
occult splatterings running
headlong   god so East

where the country grows,
& men & women
fall from trees,
great woven chord

A WINDOW'S KISS

in summertime
I'll bring sandwiches
   & we'll sit
on bent blades of grass, she says.
   if only you
were a window's
   kiss,
the knower
   still intact
& you will be
   all aural to me, you say
& I
   a symphony
in yr ear

WHAT WE MADE'S WATER

        you didn't care
about the Evidence

        you think
what we made
        's water, she says
it could've
        caved in
upon itself
        percolated the light
coned in-
        to shadows
sheer bliss
        shattering
Ontic glass
        & there you were
a mirroring

AUSTERE QUEST & CADENCE

            we are always lovers —
copper a "vertical grace" (Jay Wright)
            yr oriole
in its fundamental hour
            shares yr fugitive measure
.of
            day

it grows it retracts

            there is only ribbing
to take notice of,
            the ripples
it traces in air

            a finger sunk
into
            her ridges
of
            gown

ERR, AN INVISIBLE ESTATE

       ephemera, stolen away
to make whole,
       it cowers there
in instances

       you look down, & in the muddle,
you see new heights.
       subtle the hauntings that fall
upward
       in air
an inverted "we," our roughening,
       our invitation partial
you think the strangest thing is feeling
       this widest circumference
split

       the figures the interval the globes
of meaning you run
       parallel with

A DRINK OF LETTERS
AT ALPHABET'S EDGE

you didn't know enough of it to say, she says
little quiet space at the cusp —
you'll find me there
where I place a stone
slowing the circles
of yr reception, yr attention,
yr receptivity. It is all a drink of letters, at alphabet's edge
where they fall
like little broken vessels
where our exile is, scriptural —
yr geometries, my
ministrations.
maybe when I find it it'll be alright,
lithe breath, astral thread —
interior ampersand
& aura

THE LUCID UPWARD LADDER

            Pleiades above you, Almach
above yr bed.
            lightning in the folds of Andromeda's feet.
you can look up to Aries,
            Aldebaran, tonight not occulted
by an orange-red moon.
            she lies, you lie seeing
only whaling wheeling things
            stretching high above
their branching hair
            & heads
a spiral
            notebook

                    unthreaded, un-
          bound & with the needle,
                    turned,
          Cormorant, Perch, Eastern red cedar
                    she had made
          a constellation of it.

                    points punched through
          by a pen,
                    the paper lay in carpet.
          busy at stabbing
                    the ink head thru.
          drawing a ring,
                    she says

ECHO'S ERRAND

for Jennifer Brody

you send
    to embrace
the sweetest
    of tender sips
from yr cup
    for always

    the moving chords
moving move us
    & so the gale
& the antler horn
    the quiver nest
where I bury
    myself in yr gown

& drink of you.
                we pause
we glow
                & go out
again
                this thirst a spiral
you, I
                rest,
succumb
                to, shield to
skin of
                tally with
say, then, I'm
                yr was, yr
ipseity
                of water

NOTES

The book's epigraphs are drawn, respectively, from Jacques Derrida's preface to *Rogues: Two Essays on Reason*, Kamau Brathwaite's *Middle Passages*, and Hortense Spillers's incomparable masterpiece, "Mama's Baby, Papa's Maybe: An American Grammar Book."

The poems that compose the first section engage with, think through or alongside of, &, at times, embed titles of Cy Twombly paintings or, occasionally—as with the poems "Weightless Clutch of Sea," "Clothed in Crossroads," "Lifts an Archaic Curse," "Dazed with What We Think We Know," & "Of Shore & Grief"—the materiality of his sculptures or drawings. These poems enact a fascination, in language, or as utterance, with Twombly's color, his line's errantries, with his vanishing figures & sounds, with his sense of "history" as partial, palimpsestic, under erasure, & variously "voiced." But if Twombly is a painter of the Middle Sea, these poems conjure the *longue durée* of the Middle Passage.

Twombly once wrote, "White paint is my marble." I think, white page.

The poem "Dazed with What We Think We Know" is a rough silhouette, in language, of Twombly's haunting subtle migrations of thought in his painting, "Petals of Fire" (1989).

The poems "Upbraided, Burnt by Fire" & "Of Shore & Grief" echo, engage, allude to Twombly's "Fifty Days at Iliam" series (1978). This latter poem embeds (and tarries with) a line from Kamau Brathwaite's poem "How Europe Underdeveloped Africa."

The poem "Blown Rake of Tears" complicates, extends Twombly's painting, "Anabasis (Xenophon), 1983." I leave "four Black girls" unnamed to signal, heart-wrenchingly, the ontological totality (à la Cedric Robinson) of the event their murder was, a white settler colonial/white supremacist act of terrorism and terror. Their names are Denise McNair, Cynthia Wesley, Carole Robertson, and Addie Mae Collins, beautiful beings all. We honor them by doing the work that undoes the conditions that made their lives (incomprehensibly) targeted for what Ruth Wilson Gilmore calls "premature death." The conjuncture that is "four Black girls" and "Kitty Genovese" is a conjuring, by way of song, indebted to the gift and guide of Christina Sharpe's notion of "wake work."

The poem "In the Dark Waters Below" engages, honors, contemplates the deep porousness of Twombly's "Lepanto" series (2001).

The headnote to "Of Sea & Twisted Kelp" is from Osip Mandelstam's "Hard Night" (tr. Christian Wiman).

The epigraph to "Blue Dome" in the book's second section is drawn from Paul Celan's "Great Glowing Vault" in *Breathturn* (tr. Pierre Joris).

The reference to Jay Wright in the poem "Austere Quest &
Cadence" originates in Wright's magisterial *Music's Mask and
Measure* (2007).

ACKNOWLEDGEMENTS

My profound gratitude to the editors of the following journals and presses where earlier versions of these poems first appeared:

"Wild Lips A Wound" appeared as "From *Six Songs for Cy Twombly: VI*" in *Denver Quarterly*.

"Perception's Faraway Door," "Singed Wing," "Sheet Music," and "Dusk Water Light," first appeared, respectively, as "Shells preceding," "Silvered oval, island of glass," "Kern," and "I have poured over that" in *The Winter Anthology*.

A suite of poems from the book's first part was published as an e-chapbook by *Agape Editions/Morning House*, entitled *Shorn Ellipses*.

An earlier version of the book's second part was published as a chapbook, entitled *The Lucid Upward Ladder*, in *Verse Magazine*.

Special thanks to Janaka Stucky and Carrie Adams and to Black Ocean. A thrilling home.

Maureen Jones and Joelle Houlder cared for our children during the writing of this book. To have their love for (and stewarding of) our children conditions other possibilities for us as a family. They help *family* us. They are our family. We *family* together, which is our (and our children's) greatest gift. Thank you. Beyond words.

To Carleene Jones, Jennifer Brody, Felicia Fernandez, Fred Moten, Fanny Howe, Bill and Bev Corbett, Laura Townsend, Alessandra and Diego, Joe Donahue, Maureen Jones, Joelle Houlder, Pauline Jones, Lori Jones, Vavi Toran, Tony Van Der Meer, Lillian-Yvonne Bertram, Patrick Pritchett, J. Peter Moore, Ben Durell, Joseph Tucker Edmonds, Noam Toran, Patrick Jagoda, Ron and Rita Brody, Jason Brody, Jacob Bor, Mar Parilla, Aliza Sternstein—each of you is lyric.

All the beauty, all the love.